Ivan Doroshin

RISK SOCIETY RELIGION

Ivan Doroshin

RISK SOCIETY RELIGION

Dynamics of religious behavior in a risky reality

ScienciaScripts

Imprint

Any brand names and product names mentioned in this book are subject to trademark, brand or patent protection and are trademarks or registered trademarks of their respective holders. The use of brand names, product names, common names, trade names, product descriptions etc. even without a particular marking in this work is in no way to be construed to mean that such names may be regarded as unrestricted in respect of trademark and brand protection legislation and could thus be used by anyone.

Cover image: www.ingimage.com

This book is a translation from the original published under ISBN 978-3-8443-5032-6.

Publisher:
Sciencia Scripts
is a trademark of
Dodo Books Indian Ocean Ltd., member of the OmniScriptum S.R.L Publishing group
str. A.Russo 15, of. 61, Chisinau-2068, Republic of Moldova Europe
Printed at: see last page
ISBN: 978-620-3-05331-9

INTRODUCTION

At first glance, risk and danger seem to be something self-evident, since the corresponding perceptions are supported by society. This happens in addition to any rationalization, at the level of behavioral patterns. When discussing the topic of risk, researchers often limit themselves to educational tasks, trying to show that in their pursuit of well-being, people avoid problems, but at the same time attract even greater dangers. In E. Giddens' terminology this is called "risk of events with significant consequences"[1]. Thus, society turns out to be a "risk society", as German sociologist W. Beck formulated in his book of the same name, where decisions are forced to be made on the basis of approximate assessments. "Future situations," writes F. Knight, "to which we adapt our behavior usually depend on the behavior of a huge number of objects and are caused by so many factors that we do not try to take them all into account. Exact knowledge, however, is theoretically only possible when our sphere of interest is strictly limited to those aspects of the object's behavior that are determined by its physical parameters, and such knowledge can only be obtained by using complex laboratory methods[2].

Another opportunity for the researcher is to explore different types of risk assessment and risk attitudes in different societies and cultures[3]. Perhaps the most interesting type of risk assessment is the religious variant, which in turn becomes no less interesting object of attention of a risk researcher. Thus, our task is a socio-philosophical "verbalization" of attitudes to the risk of religious communities as a separate option for risk assessment.

The basic parcels can be marked as follows:

- Religion is a "sacred subject": in its most perfect and most imperfect form, this area of social practice deserves the highest respect (M. Muller).

---

[1] Giddens, E. Fate, Risk and Security // THESIS: Theory and History of Economic and Social Institutions and Systems. Ep. 5: Risk, uncertainty, randomness, - 1994. - C. 110.
[2] Knight F. The concept of risk and uncertainty // TESIS. Episode. 5. - 1994. C 12.
[3] See: Ibid. - C. 107.

- It is possible to study behavior motivated by transcendent beliefs without discussing the reality of the transcendent.

- Only the social practices of transcending give an idea of the rule in religious behavior;

- It is necessary to distinguish between religion as a specific human phenomenon and religious behavior, as a universal characteristic of life. Religious belief is a reaction based on a system of reflex arcs grouped in such a way that some statements and statements can be positively reinforced (W. Wells)[4].

Religious behavior, used today mainly as a concept of psychology of religion, is known, however, to the philosophical horizon of behaviorism. Within the framework of the topic mentioned in the title, religious behavior is presented as nothing but "socialized" transcendence.

The term "religion" in sociology often refers to both religion itself and religious behavior, which is controversial from the standpoint of a philosophical study of religious experience. It is necessary to limit and concretize the concepts.

Religious behavior is a type of behavior that promotes adaptation to the environment *and survival*, a factor in the optimization of biological processes. Religion is understood as a congenital predisposition, which was formed as a result of natural selection. Attention should be paid to the *social potential of* religious behavior for survival, which is especially important for risk science, as well as allows philosophy to actively engage in the study of these problems[5].

Riscology may be interested in finding the prerequisites of faith proposed by behaviorism[6]. These are the primary instincts (parental care, curiosity, running away, self-abasement), as well as emotions (surprise, fear, negative sense of self, tenderness). There is a direct value of faith for survival because of its optimizing biological impact on human beings: "The fact that religious faith exists among primitive peoples everywhere clearly demonstrates its value for *survival processes*[7]. But if we are talking

---

[4] См.: Wells, W.R. The Biological Foundation of Beliefs. - S.L. - 1921. - P. 6.
[5] Afanasyev, I.A. Philosophical foundations of the theory of social risks. - Saratov, 2006. - C. 17.
[6] See: Wells, W.R. Op. cit.
[7] See: Ibid.

about *human survival*, we can probably talk about the power of the *optimizing social impact of* religion on human beings. It is necessary to teach the religions of children, college students - idealistic philosophy is not because of the obligatory truth, but because of its usefulness[8]. Thus, we can talk about the non-metaphysical contribution of religion to the foundation of social security. It seems that metaphysics as a language practice hardly corresponds with riscology, therefore, it is necessary to abandon both metaphysical language and even introspective description. We have come to the *limit of information assimilation*, the "language limit" (P.L. Kapitsa). This also applies to the limit of metaphysical discourse. This seems to be the most important characteristic of religion in a *risk society*.

Studying the "inner side" of religion is largely meaningless:

1. The introspection brings us into the field of theology;
2. Because of the discursive boundaries of philosophy as a scientific discipline;
3. The sociality of a study requires at least an interpersonal dimension;
4. The position is consistent with the notion of the super significance for religion of the interpersonal dimension in Christian Orthodoxy ("love" as the maxim of religious conduct), which can be called the starting point for analyzing the religious behavior of a European;
5. In practice we are dealing with *interiorization - the* doctrine is known to believers and perceived as a system of their own "inner" values, is the foundation of their "inner" religiosity. The system of religious socialization leads to the development of patterns of "internal" religiosity. Their development is the ultimate goal of the system.

Thus, the selection processes have a kind of "negative valence" for the subject due to their risk, unreliability, high price for their implementation, while the religiousness of the behavioral reaction is usually determined by the "positive valence" in the situation of choice. Thus, this is where we meet the essence and the most interesting phenomena.

---

[8] See: Ibid.

Chapter 1: DEFINITIONS OF RELIGIOUS DISCUSSIONS OF PHILOSOF SCIENCES RISK

1.1. Structural changes in religious behavior within a risk society

Images of risk and algorithms for overcoming it have belonged for thousands of years to the world of religion and religious behavior. Everything connected with - uncertainty, with unforeseen circumstances, possible failures, causing fear and desire to avoid undesirable consequences, as well as the action of unpredictable natural or social forces is sacralized. In other words, all this requires special training - the environment of the sanctified, as well as the desecrated ("ambivalence" of the sacral contained in the - etymology of the word). If we proceed from the concept of animism as a minimum of religion (E. Taylor), then a shaman is an "expert of chance" called to explain everything unheard of and to oppose it (K.-G. Jung).

The risk society has given birth to a cult of experts and specialists: they perform functions that in the past were perfectly performed by the army, police and church. This new "shamanism", unprecedented in the world, requires more and more victims. Ordinary consciousness is unable to reproduce either the normal space of the profane or the normal religious behavior, which is associated with the concept of ritual and rhythm. The space-time continuum is deformed. The "unfitness" of space and time is characteristic of the sacralized state, as the folklore time of 33-year one-way journey with 3-day return, as the transformation of space with a comb-forest, mirror-lake.

In social terms, it affects the level of legitimization of elites (through sacralization) and power structures. The dominance of the elites, as the dominance of "atamans" in the periods of Russian history's turmoil, leads to the impossibility of reproducing the profiled and *existential fatigue,* and, consequently, to unpreparedness for the risk situation. Thirst for status deforms the usual life from the stand and requires an incredible tension of human forces.

Our task is to define what terms meant the risks in the world's religious traditions, and to designate parallels in the discourse of risk society, with the maximum exclusion of metaphysical definitions. In addition, it is necessary to identify and take into account the accentuation of risk situations. Risk is associated with the risk of material losses, and less often - with the loss of *trust*. In the case of secular consciousness, the former is more important, while in the case of religious consciousness, the latter is determined by the loss of trust as the basis of religious life.

Both the "privacy of escape from risk" and "globality" (something like "super-sociality") obscure the social nature of risk, the social causes or social consequences of risks remain unclear. Common sense, though, deliberately regulating the daily life of events, evades the value perception of risk. Thus, alternative options - religious systems - become relevant. As such, they exist in the space of modern society.

Risk is generally recognized as an opportunity for success, so there is an opportunity to discuss "inadequate riskiness" and "inadequate care". Thus, the most important characteristic is the connotation of risk associated with its history. Interestingly, the biblical methanarrativ is a chain of unique situations, a kind of *school of inevitable choice*.

Riscologists talk about a continuous increase in states of uncertainty (V.B. Ustiantsev), about the social need to obtain professional knowledge. But, despite the "professionalization" and profiling of risks, in practice, in a situation of inevitable choice and serious crisis, an ordinary Russian turns to... parish priest.

The subject of the disciplinary study are risks expressed in symbolic meanings and concept lines of specific scientific disciplines. We are interested in the case of expression in symbolic meanings. Conceptual rows of specific disciplines specifically dealing with risk issues are quite young, and symbolic reinforcements remain.

The conceptual spectrum of risk is represented by disciplinary studies, symbolic series remain, but the problem remains *categorical risk measurement* (space and time of risk), without which serious analysis of potential states of social objects is impossible.

Christian versions of social concepts are based on the idea of original sin, as a total "damage" to the nature of the world, which has naturally affected social relations. It is interesting that the Muslim doctrine fundamentally denies the original sin, quite idealistically imagining the social world as a natural state. Such an attitude is fraught with unpredictable risks. Total splitting of a community representative must be real in the consciousness of a believer and is usually the main source of the problem. Nevertheless, the concept of "humility" in Orthodox Christianity and "submission" in righteous Islam is that "fertile ground" (the Greek equivalent of the word "humility" is translated as such) for working on the problems of "global communities" of the Christian Church and the Muslim Ummah.

Risky reality as a manifestation of social reality generates and re-structures the sources of social risks. Therefore, it is possible to assume the restructuring of "reinforcements" of religious behavior within the confines of a confession. In practice, we are dealing not with pure confessional or ethnic behavior, but with *an ethno-confessional alloy,* which is being restructured. Even pseudo-ethno-confessionalism is able to quickly restructure and produce new risks. For example, the North Caucasus gangs have shifted from protruding national protest to a slogan that can be conveyed in a similar way: A "righteous" foreigner is the best friend, while a "wrong" Vainakh is the worst enemy. That is why the police have suffered much more than federal units over the past year.

Pseudo-religious organizations offer nothing more than their "risk management", easily producing virtual risks, bringing the community to a state of manageable hysteria. In addition, the individual finds himself under the pressure of unsuccessful decisions or changed circumstances. Such associations are characterized not by community, but by corporate *behavior*. Interestingly, the space of the winning corporate style is the Japanese civilization - our closest neighbor, "distributed" between the Rebusinto sects, as well as "traditional" and non-traditional Buddhist sects.

Today the attention of ricologists is focused on three factors of social dynamics: technological, organizational and environmental. In the language of religious systems, the concepts of "ritual", "community" and "salvation" correspond to them. Pseudo-religiousity is also based on religious behavior. Accordingly, there is a basis for the formation of three types of sects: *technological* - the proposed "technique of salvation", often with images of cosmonautics and other variants of pseudo-popularization of science, *organizational* - "salvation" at the expense of a "special organization", where a person is attracted by the one who says the word "we"; *ecological - the* most pseudo-tolerant organizations with free membership, as a rule, are non-language.

Interestingly, this is not only about organizations and movements that are - registered and identified as religious. The problem is much deeper. Religious behavior is exploited in a "risk society" by a variety of organizations. Sometimes they can be easily identified as a cult of goods (MLM systems, etc.) Especially it is typical for the corporate style of behavior.

Thus, in a "risk society" religious behavior is exploited by non-religious - organizations.

1.2. Crisis of rational strengthening of faith in risk society

Collective decisions of risk subjects often generate not only new risks, but also a crisis of rational support of faith. The more "mass" the choice becomes, the less it requires rationality in justifying action. This pattern is actively used in social advertising, popularization and missionary work. Active actions of risk subjects do not always contain rational attitudes. Technological improvement overcomes the established logical and social acceptability of risk (Beck W.)[9] . Thus, the subrational and super-rational layer of substantiation of "risk manager" decisions is actualized, although the terms "subrationality" and "super-rationality" require some explanation: "There are things that will always be a *challenge to* thought, because thought can only capture them by the method of instruction. For example, the challenge to thought is "here," "here," and "now. This is the sphere of subrational, i.e., what is below the thought. And the challenge to thought is the "Who", i.e., the ontology of personal being. This is the sphere of the super-rational[10]. Perhaps, we are talking not only about a challenge to thought, but about any *challenge*. Where the situation can be solved by pure calculus, is it possible to talk about risk? We can, but such situations do not exist. The usual rational structures of trust experience a crisis, it becomes a source of uncertainty that "life will continue" (E. Giddens), but this is not a momentary fear - life itself becomes a hostage of human

---

[9] See: Beck, W. Risk Society. On the Way to Another Modern. - M., - 2000.
[10] Duplinskaya, Yu.M. Ontological basis of differences between theology and philosophy // Pimenov Readings. - Saratov, - 2007. - C. 67.

projects.

Religious communities of modern times are characterized by anonymous institutions and social systems, the legitimization of which is irrational. They complement each other, create a very fluid "probabilistic structure" of public life and are integrated into a risk society. To a greater extent, this phenomenon seems to apply to Muslim communities, which is caused by some attitudes towards "unproblematic". It is known that a Muslim community, as a rule, does not like to talk about its problems outside (unlike Christians). This attitude is perfectly expressed by the phrase I heard in a private conversation: "What problems can Islam have? It is not customary to talk about a neighbor who deviates from the norms, one should talk about the right Muslim. On the one hand, the situation is not only convenient, but also productive - everything is clear and obvious. Is a "wrong" Muslim a believer at all?

In addition, religious behavior presupposes the existence of permanent and temporary risk zones (marked as "sacred" or "sacred"), where non-rationalized crisis-value rules are in place, generating social tension and destabilizing existing social structures. These zones can be nothing but a sphere of geopolitical interests. Knowledge of the sacralization mechanism is essential for the integrated management of risky territories.

Modernity also represents a split in technological rationality of "organized irresponsibility" (W. Beck)[11]. The change of envelopes corresponds to a general paradigm shift in philosophical paradigm - away from Newtonian mechanical schemes. The new conventions differ from the mechanistic perception of the world, as the Prigogin pendulum differs from that of Newton. The cargo in Prigorjin's pendulum is not suspended, but placed on a rod. It will "fall" out of balance and become a different type of system. Any changes here are irreversible. The widespread scheme of rational/irrational in the understanding of religion should be replaced by more productive conventions, typical for the beginning of the XXI century - responsibility, trust, risk-solidarity, capable of localizing risks.

The virtualization of religion makes a new, unexpected contribution to the crisis

---

[11] See: Beck, W. Edict, op. cit.

of rational strengthening of faith in a risk society. In Russia, these are challenges not - only to the leading communities - Orthodoxy and Sunni Islam, but also new problems for their relations. Virtualization exacerbates the struggle between the desire for freedom and willingness to comply with the requirements of social order, and forms the field of specific risky actions of individuals in the space of Orthodox, Protestant and Muslim business ethics.

The crisis of rational strengthening of faith in the risk society is also manifested in the fact that the humanist discourse in modern civilization intersects with the image on the screen of the most bloody shootings of disasters and tragedies. Isn'humanist discourse? Humanist discourse itself already raises questions - why talk about humanity so much? Is it so clearly missing? On the other hand, why talk so much about danger and risks? Maybe they are also so obviously missing, and we are dealing with pseudo-risks, even "pseudo-risks factory" and simulation? "Religious" terrorism and ecological - disaster are the tops of verbal heaps in mass media and science. What can an ordinary person do to solve these "problems"? Terror never leaves a choice.

Risk is possible with rational reinforcement, otherwise we are more likely to - deal with danger. The infantile inhabitant often simply lacks risk, perhaps because of irrational attraction of will. All her efforts are aimed at preserving, paradoxically, the infantile perception. It is very telling that there is a mass passion for trance techniques, and for the sake of trance itself. Interestingly, the use of techniques of religious traditions for their own sake leads to regression, because it leads not to change, but to - consolidation and subsequent dominance of the state. This pattern can be explained by the example of combat operations, with which, by the way, many traditions compare - religious life (spiritual scolding, etc.): a situation where the war is conducted for the sake of war, followed by the consolidation of the military dictatorship. Possible "occupation" of all other areas of human life, which is passed off as spiritual life. Self-manipulation in this case is possible because of a typical mistake - spiritual life is considered an end in itself by many people who lead a religious life. It is forgotten that the life of the spirit is not the merit of man, but only the restoration of broken bonds - religion ("re-" return particle, "ligo" - to unite).

Preservation of narcissism in social life requires even greater efforts, including the fight against rationality, which is also very similar to the risk. Not only does an average citizen lack risk, he or she is not capable of it. Pseudo-risks seem to be camouflaged dangers; to find risk among them is the first task. The screen feed increases the game moment of perception or directly creates it, as in the case of terror. The game presentation of danger also does not mean risk, but perhaps it is a technique of manipulation.

By "posing" danger, a person "swells up to the figure of the lord of the earth"[12]. He becomes nothing more than a *dangerous object* himself, which seems to be the exact opposite of real *risk*. Maybe this is the ambivalence of human nature? At least, a person has always treated his body as a dangerous object, hence all sorts of taboo techniques. Man misses something essential for existence itself, trying to compensate for the reverse course of thought: if existence eludes us because of the absence of something essential for it, then we will grasp what is dangerous to existence, the danger itself. Thus, the - substitution of risk with danger occurs, which is perhaps the most important technique of manipulating consciousness in contemporary social practices.

It is interesting that for religion, a person is not self-identified, that is, the size equal to his body, his behavior, even the sum of the individual. Rather, it represents a project. Orthodox Christianity, for example, tells us about the mystery of a *person, -* incomprehensible to individuality and even to *a person* (lat. "mask", first of all - social, glorious equivalent of "harya" - mask of a skomoroch). Where there is a personality - it is impossible to define it, simply because it is always an identity of behavior. This is the secret of the Christian confession. Even the "sinner" (a person of total distorted - behavior) is called because he is not equal to a set of behavioral skills and preferences, passions. "Sin" is just a "slip-up", as translated literally from the Greek "Arjartpra".

It is necessary to determine the risk, based not only on anthropogenic and other factors external to a person, but first of all on human, personal measurements of possible risk level[13]. The key schemes of risk understanding in historical perspective were

---

[12] Heidegger, M. Question about technology // Heidegger, M. Time and being. M., - 1993. C. 233.
[13] See: Babosov, E.M. Risk Civilization // http://www.ubrus.org/dictionary-units. Address to the resource:

outlined by N. Luman[14]: not only courage and fear, but also sin and pride. The concept of loss is not found in religious systems, and religious behavior is unsuccessful. In some systems, for example in Islam, even evil is relative.

Religion does not mean that you are risking anything, in fact, you can't take anything with you, and therefore you can't risk anything. Therefore, the risk concerns only those relationships in which things can be excluded. We fear because we have too many "values": "Blessed are the poor in spirit" (Mt 5:3). On the contrary, modus "to be" is characterized by values that no one can take away: "For they are the kingdom of heaven" (Mt 5:3). A clear offer to give up security in favor of risk can be seen in the Bible sentence: "Then He (Jesus) said to them, 'But now, whoever has a sack, take it, and also the sum; and whoever has not, sell your clothes and buy a sword' (Luk. 22:36). Interestingly, the cutting tool has always symbolized rationality.

"A man is braver than a plant" (A.V. Mikhailov)[15], but in practice, a man, not having a support in himself, begins to look for it outside himself, becoming a "plant". He decides that the meaning of life is in the "service" of the nation, in "religion," in wealth, in the "beloved" person, etc. In terms of existential phenomenology, this is ontologically unsafe. Fanaticism is a pre-religious behavior, generated by fear of risk.

Religious behavior implies the establishment of new social ties and the transition of existing ones to a qualitatively new level. Pseudo-religiousity leads to the breakup of social ties. "The risk is as follows: if a person experiences another as having free will, he is defenseless against the possibility of experiencing himself as the object of his experience, and thus the feeling of his own subjectivity disappears. A person is afraid of the possibility to become nothing more than a thing in the world of another person who does not have his own life, his own being[16]. The religious systems of the Abrahamicheska tradition make different accents in the notions of social connections. The other person is not experienced as having a completely free will, hence "Judge not, let not you be judged" (Matthew 7:1).

04.02.10.
[14] Luman, N. The concept of risk // THESIS, - 1994. - Episode. 5. - C. 157.
[15] Mikhailov, A.V. Heidegger. A man in the world. - M., - 1990. - C. 42.
[16] In the same place. - C. 43.

The religious type of social behavior tends to search for *its* solutions and failures. Interestingly, even social events that do not have a source of human individuality are not alienated, but are mastered. However, instead of a discourse of responsibility (*religious tradition*), there is a danger of engaging in a discourse of guilt (*fundamentalism*). Such a substitution can be committed purposefully as part of a manipulation mechanism. There is a certain pattern: ecumenists are usually believers brought up in an extremely strict religious community. A good example is the life of Fr. A good example is the life of Father Alexander I, who was brought up in an extremely harsh manner of the so-called Catacomb Church. "External" conditions, as a rule, relate to the divine Providence: the "incarnate cross" in Christianity, the will of God in Islam, etc. The fundamentalists are converts, past period of God-seeking, brought up in liberal - conditions. The external conditions are extremely controversial - the sources of problems are either imperfect and unfair social conditions, or directly hostile intrigue and conspiracies ("Zionists", "kafirs", "blacks", "Americans", "freemasons", "ecumenists", etc.) The use of such labels is akin to magical practices - having defined the "enemy" one can not be afraid of him, the surrounding becomes more "understandable" - the most important function of magic is protection from "chaos". There is also the social purpose of the conspiracy - association, in this case - a sense of unity. As a result, the image of gangs (terrorist and extremist groups, ethnic OCGs, - economic - corruption groups and syndicates, etc.) is either smeared or camouflaged. Guilt is transferred to the population, partly "dissolving", partly accumulating - causing a bouquet of guilt, protest, resentment, charging the marked communities with new energy, which is perfectly used by fundamentalism.

Thus, we have tried to trace the crisis of rational reinforcement of faith from behavioral reactions to "ontological security", which is experienced by everyone due to the fact of life, movement forward, the threat of emptiness and meaninglessness, and the fear of death. Fatal moments threaten to break through the protective 'cocoon' that provides individual ontological security, as the 'common thing' attitude that is so important to this cocoon inevitably breaks down [17]. The individual's desire for ontological security is manifested by a compulsive desire for mastery of things, social actors by irrational mastery of space. As for the perception of time, the most mysterious and intimate act for a religious person, such mastery means "throwing it away" to the future - where it will take place. The world of risk is that "now", as well as being, according to Zen, for example, requires admiration for the eternal "now"[18]. The last word is "This!" [19].

1.3. Religious Anthropology about the Risk of Present and Desired Condition

According to the ironic statement of VS Solovyov, "man is a monkey and therefore is called to implement the kingdom of good on earth[20]. The model of man and the mistakes of "modelers" can be very expensive. For example, the anthropological - ideal of the "man-cosmonaut" in the Soviet Union "auctioned off" in a pseudo-religious search for perestroika man - there were a lot of people willing to go out into the open "astral" or to experience unity with a certain cosmos. The mismatch between a given goal and the reality - to be an astronaut and never become one - can lead to a variety of deviations in social practices.

The first thing to note is that the ideal of a man of religious tradition is real; moreover, he will achieve it - saints, reverends, righteous people, etc. Perhaps, the most interesting material for discussion of anthropological risks is Christian orthodoxy. If sin is a prototype of the concept of risk in the religious picture of the world, it is the doctrine of sin that sets an interesting vector for research, especially the doctrine of original sin - a doctrine that, incidentally, is not present in Islam.

Schematically, we outline the doctrine of Orthodox Christianity about man. St. Isaac the Syrian points to three human states[21]:

1.   natural, in which it is created, *fragile*;

2.   natural, in which it is located;

---

[17] Giddens, E. Fate, Risk and Safety // THESIS. - № 5. - 1994. - C. 10.
[18] See: Suzuki, D. Basics of Zen Buddhism. - Reverse. Almanac. - St. Petersburg, 1992.
[19] See: Teacher Ganto, Blue Rock Records // Nisker, V. Crazy Wisdom. St. Petersburg: Peter, 2001.
[20] Frank, S.L. Reality and man. - M., 1997. - C. 334.
[21] See: Isaac Sirin, St. Words ascetic. - M., 1993.

3.   supernatural, to which it is called, *strong*.

Man in his natural state did not have an experienced knowledge of who he is on his *own*, without God. Lack of knowledge has become a ground for falling into sin, a man without God is nothing. It is interesting that Christianity says about irreversible - processes. Human nature once split into three autonomous parts: mind (source of thought), heart (source of feelings) and body. Hence the interest in irreversible social processes in the horizon of Christian philosophy in both Western and Eastern tradition. I.A. Krylov wrote a wonderful fable 'Swan, Cancer and Pike' about human disorder. Christian anthropology is a wonderful key to European literature and art, but both in Russia are still trying to teach outside the Christian context. Thus, the *mind is* incapable of learning the Higher Truth, filled with the earthly (lowly); "from the *heart* come evil thoughts, murder, adultery, theft, perjury, blasphemy" (Matthew 15:19); the *body is* subject to fatigue, suffering, illness, death. V.N. Lossky writes: "The hierarchy in man is upside down. Spirit was to live by God, soul by spirit, body by soul. But the spirit begins to parasitize on the soul'. The soul, in turn, becomes a parasite of the body - passions rise. And finally, the body becomes a parasite of the earthly universe, kills to eat, and so finds death[22]. The damaged state, which has both anthropological and social projections, in Orthodox theology is called the original sin. Man has become mortal - that is, he can "fall apart", disintegrate in life. In the horizon of cultural studies there is a concept of "schizz culture". *In* order to change the state, a person should make an *effort*[23], which may even be considered unnatural by an inhabitant.

Thus, let us try to highlight the components of religious behavior in a situation of risk: initiation by threat, irreversibility of processes, effort. Being in a risk situation seems to be assessed positively: "When the pot is heated by fire, neither a fly nor anything else reptiles can touch it; when it cools down, then they sit on it. The same happens to a man: as long as he is in the spiritual business, the enemy can not hit him"

---

[22] Lossky, V.N. Essay of Mystical Theology of the Eastern Church. - M., - 1991. - C. 253.
[23] "From the days of John the Baptist to the present day, the kingdom of heaven is taken by force, and those who use force delight him" (Matthew 11:12); "The law and the prophets before John; from now on, the kingdom of God is good, and by every force enters it" (Luke 16:16).

(Abba Pimen)[24]. Naturally, such a "positive valence", if necessary, generates an active "sociality", an example of which is the activity of St. Sergius of Radonezh, St. Alexander Nevsky, St. Innocent, Metropolitan of Moscow and many others).

The most important socially important characteristic is "humility" - "positive valence", a situation of openness and acceptance - is also a condition for taking risk. "Retribution (but) is not about virtues (*Catholicism*) or labor (*Protestantism),* but about humility born of them. If this is not the case, all the virtues and all the labors are in vain" (St. Isaac the Syrian).

The concept of "sin" may indeed find itself in a descriptive series of risk situations (N. Luman), but it seems that one cannot unambiguously reduce one to another. If sin is a "mistake", then "passion" is no longer translated, because - it's just an indication of the suffering bail - "it's not me who lives, but me who lives".

Lack of security also manifests itself in the fact that a person opposes the inner reality of consciousness to the body[25]. Interestingly, starting with the Christian doctrine of salvation (which also applies to the transformation of the body), religious consciousness does not oppose the body of internal reality in Orthodox Christianity. Although the platonic idea of the body as a prison of the soul will still disturb mankind, the concept of the "saved" body, perhaps even the "tool" of salvation in Christian Orthodoxy sets a different vector of philosophy. The body is no longer perceived as a source of "nasty" (in any sense) and cause of "death. The problem of the vessel - half full and half empty - is solved in favor of optimists. Man - the "vessel of God" is not half dead, but rather "half" saved: if Adam's "sin" is "washed" by Christ, the second component of "salvation" is required, the synergy (God and man) - the movement of man to salvation. The "feat of Jesus" thus puts man in a situation of risk - and ontological. It should be noted that this is not an attempt to speak on behalf of the Christian Church or theology, the author rather tries to understand and describe philosophically.

Human morality is also a source of danger. It is like a pendulum of classical

---

[24] See: A kindness chosen by the lay people. - Purification Monastery Edition, 1999.
[25] See: Malkina, S.M. Philosophical Anthropology of Risk // Introduction to Social Riscology. - Saratov, 2010.

mechanics, the load has fallen down, ethical swings set it in motion only for a while - the state is stable and it is fully in its world, self-sufficient. Interestingly, Christianity has painfully hit the established moral foundations - in the New Testament it is called "the elders' legends" (Mar. 7:3), "the human legend" (Mar. 7:8). Christianity in the Roman Empire was described as "scandalous" ("uncompromising"). Interestingly, the Roman "tolerance" granted by the state was completely alien to religious behavior. Long patience leads to quick problems. Tolerance is the rejection of a situation of risk, a search for security out of choice. Religious systems offer a different conceptual range - love, humility, submission, patronage, finally, etc. The concept of tolerance is an - attempt to place religious behavior in the "bed" of classical mechanics.

Traditionally, it is believed that in the conditions of a group there is a - transformation of responsibility in the direction of reducing its personal measure (the - phenomenon of "diffusion of responsibility"[26]), which leads to an increase in the risk of group decisions. It is interesting that the reduction of group decision risk level is achieved in religious systems by increasing personal responsibility through the concepts of "sin", "righteousness", "court", etc.

[27]Grinning's four "challenges" have been perfectly supported by religious - behavior for at least the last two thousand years of sustainable human existence. The - conclusion from Grinning is that danger is guaranteed. Moreover, as existentialists explain, we are guaranteed to die. The basis for religious behavior is thus made clear: not to take a risk? Should we not seek eternal life? "Faith" as a state, apparently, indicates a situation of cognitive risk:

1) Limited reason for making a "final" decision, hence the freedom of knowledge;

2. Recognition of the limited "ontological" resource, thrown into the limits of space and time, hence the inability to refuse to make a decision.

The study of the fundamental bases of behavioral reactions in the conditions of risk has come to reject unilateral interpretation of risk in the context of thoughtlessly in the direction of constructive interpretation. In this case, riskiness is directly related to the

---

[26] See: Karpov, A.V. Psychology of group decisions. - M, - 2000. - C. 358.
[27] См.: Greening, T. Existential challenges and responces // The Humanistic Psychologist. - 1992, vol. 20. - № 1, pp.111-115.

worldview and critical function of religion.

Functional analysis of risky behaviors is defined not only by the resolution of dangerous situation with the focus on the possibility of failure, but also as the ability to calculate, determine the situation, as well as the ability to model and even transform it in accordance with their goals. Hope turns into confidence and experience of the state of faith: "Muscles come into a state of full coordination, its neurons are organized into specific patterns, the activity of its glands is in close interaction with all other organic processes in such a way that their total organization is as close as possible to the one that will prevail when the expected event actually occurs[28]. Thus, faith is a "school" of - behavioral reactions under risk conditions, in the context of its *constructive* - interpretation.

1.4. Terrorism - "winning" painful topic of social philosophy

The real impulse in the development of risk sociology was the pseudo-Lama threat, which had a great influence on the models of "risk society". [29]The question is clearly posed: "As a result of what processes is a religious culture capable of reproducing terrorist risks? This is a clear and interesting position, but can a religious culture reproduce terror as well as culture in general?

If risk is the ultimate use of favorable opportunities in an unfavorable situation[30], if there is a free, negative or creative act[31], then the combination of "terrorist risk" used must be explained, it does not seem to be an established one. The risk of terrorism - as a dilemma of social creativity and terror is still clear, but... Based on the above definitions, it is also unclear: "Terrorism as a form of fundamental risk produced in the religious sphere has become a satellite of globalization. Globalization gave birth to terrorism as a global threat and at the same time received a crushing blow from it. The feeling of danger, of risk has become universal"[32]. Terrorism is indeed a threat, although it is considered global by a European who is used to seeing his life as global. The sense

---

[28] Wulff, D.M. Psyhology of Religion: Classic and Contemporary Views. - N. Y., - 1997. - P. 114-115.

[29] Orlov, M.O. Risks of global dynamics: religion and terrorism // www.ru. Address to the resource: 04.02.10.

[30] See: Filimonova, O.F. Historical preconditions of modern theory of risk formation // Introduction to social risk science. - Saratov, 2010.

[31] See: Malkina S.M. op. cit.

[32] See: Orlov. Op. cit.

of danger has become truly universal, but as you can see, only a feeling. One can disagree with the question of the emergence of terrorism by globalization, because the organized terror has not only been known since Carthage, it usually pursues far from global goals.

One cannot but agree that often "science does not reduce risk, but exacerbates - risk awareness" (N. Luman). By escalating the risk, it pours water on the mill of terror. "Security", only "like" classical resources, becomes one of the socially organized consumer goods, a product of the security industry, in other words, "values" of induced hysteria. Parallelism with real threats, for example, some environmental threats - usually a sign of weak arguments for the "risk of terrorism" and a direct reference to manipulation of consciousness. The strength of terrorism is its constant calling. Armed clashes in the North Caucasus with a clear crossroads of nationalism/terrorism have demonstrated the potential of *virtual weapons*: terrorism as a virtual replication of banditry. Terrorism is a "psychological" product, rather a behavioral, easily replicable behavioral product.

Networking risks and religion is a very interesting topic. Completely new properties of religious behavior are found in *communicative risks,* because in the communicative space the mental structures and values of individuals enter into complex interactions with "informational" institutionalization.

"Globalization, penetrating into the world of traditional religions, aggravates - internal contradictions: exacerbates the degradation of political systems, the collapse of moral values, the collapse of the family. Nowhere does it produce such a destructive - effect as in the Islamic world[33]. It is interesting that Muslims perfectly assimilate liberal values to position themselves in the world of liberal values, not liberal values, but "liberal values for...". They use the achievements of Western civilization quite correctly, without trying to destroy their own identity with their help. In France, a Muslim woman will fight for the right to wear the hijab just as a civil right. This is not a double standard, but a quite rational attitude worth learning.

It is quite rightly noted that "traditional religious cultures such as Islam are too

---

[33] See: Orlov. Op. cit.

serious to take the fruits of modern civilization with humor or unconditional tolerance. Therefore, they are often perceived with hatred and rejection. There is a risk of violent justice being done in the name of an authoritarian religious idea. It is Islam that is capable of becoming a global political system, offering an alternative version of globalization"[34] . Interestingly, Islam, which emerged in an urban environment, is now associated with "village identity" ("the essence of Islam is the restoration of communal (village) identity as opposed to personal or national identity")[35].

Strange as it may seem, a community that aspires to a risk-free existence inevitably comes to terror. This also applies to religious organizations, both in the Christian and Muslim world. The Christian Church of post-fascist Europe can help the Muslim scholarly world save this world from the temptations of risk-free "bliss" in a situation of "open gates" of Muslim thought.

Thus, the thesis of global terrorist risks seems to proceed from the understanding of religious behavior as the activity of losers from changes, who are afraid of the new global world. It is impossible to unequivocally agree with the statement: People are being saved from the economic uncertainty of their real world," Thoreau writes, "by retreating to the confidence of *some* religious world, where they are told that if they obey the prescribed rules, they will be saved[36]. The texts on terrorism are mostly sociological - at least in the sense of worshipping sociological knowledge, but it is also necessary to - look critically at the situation.

Terrorism has nothing to do with religious behavior, based on the positions mentioned in Section 1. It is a pseudo-religious motivation. It poses a huge threat to religious communities, jeopardizing religious understanding in general. As a result, religious behavior is increasingly perceived as *deviant*! Not surprisingly, the negative reaction of the average person to teaching Orthodox culture in school is not surprising, as is the widespread perception of mosques as centers of recruitment of extremists.

The purpose of terrorism is to destroy community consciousness through fear and

---

[34] See: Orlov. Op. cit.

[35] See: Ibid.

[36] Thoreau, L. The Future of Capitalism. How today's economic forces are shaping tomorrow's world. - Novosibirsk, - 1999. - C. 278.

mistrust, as the basis of community behavior is *joint security* with openness to any risks of modernity. Thus, it is possible to explain the meaning of the word "salvation" in a non-physical way. If terrorists deliberately and openly put religious slogans and religious behavior in general under attack of journalism, then isn't this one of the most important goals of modern terrorism. Instead of community behavior, behavior is offered rather as corporate thinking.

Interestingly, the Muslim interpretation of social life is closer to liberal Europe than to Christian one. The state, embodying the principles of institutional liberalization, may also demonstrate aggression towards the so-called "undemocratic environment".

So, it should be noted in conclusion:

1. The situation of danger and the risk situation may coincide in space and time, but this is not a reason to identify them;
2. There are two states preceding behavioral reactions: risk taking and risk aversion (attempts to hide, search for "strength" beyond ontological strength); they are successfully recorded in religious behavior;
3. Two variants of behavioral reactions based on the nature of the previous state were recorded in systems of religious behavior: "piety" and "sinfulness" ("goodness" and "depersonalization" of philosophical discourse);

Several possible directions should be indicated as a research prospect:

1. Analysis of social risks in global communities: network risks of religious behavior, virtualization of social threats.
2. Development of theoretical constructions of social risks taking into account the - specifics of religious behavior.

The development of religious behavior risks falls within the sphere of risk conceptualization. This work is necessary both in social philosophy and in sociology of - religion. Overcoming the ordinary or narrowly-disciplinary understanding of risk society, philosophical discourse makes it possible to identify the systemic nature of risks from the perspective of the problem of social ambivalence, to establish a link between the concepts of intellectual and religious risk.

Chapter 2: RELIGIOUS COMMUNICATION IN RICOGICAL REALITY: categorical analysis

2.1. The problem of defining religious communities

Social interests and needs for professional knowledge about the risks of religious behavior are dictated by the ricogeneity of religious communities and institutions, as well as the inseparability of the problems of religious behavior risks in riscology, for example, the mixing of practices of religious communities with magical behavior. In addition, the crisis of risk math has aroused interest in the risk ontology[37]. The ontological risk dimension also defines the religious community. "The products of human thought necessary to preserve and maintain a common essence (gemeinsames Wesen).... find their end in such important forms as community (Gemeinde), state, *church*, often mistaken for elements of reality and sometimes for something supernatural[38].

The purpose of this small section is to highlight the range of questions - concerning categorical analysis of religious communities in situations of risk. The problem is among the topical issues and suggests answers to the questions: what is "religious community" as a socio-philosophical category? What is the difference between the concept of "religious system"? why does the concept apply to metaphysics, rather than organization of the human community? How do these categories relate to the definition of "social governance"?

Interestingly, "the way in which social things or individuals exist is no different from the way in which gods are imagined, thought and created by linked people, whether in the image of animals, in a human image or in an image that combines the features of animals and the face of the century, in order to worship them"[39].

The need to use the term "religious community" was due to several reasons. First, the use of religious knowledge in social philosophy based on the study of the

---

[37] Luman, N. Social Systems: An Essay on General Theory // 3-Western Theoretical Sociology of the 80s. Reference Collection. - M., 1989. - C. 41-64.
[38] Tennis, F. Generality and Society // Sociological Journal. - 1998. - №3/4. - C. 207.
[39] In the same place. C. 210.

systemic nature of religious communities. Secondly, in the conditions of - democratization of society, non-governmental organizations also became more actively involved in power relations, and in this regard, the problem of institutionalization of religious communities in the space of civil society arises. Third: the introduction of the systemic approach was conditioned by the search for universal regularities and mechanisms that would provide society with stability and survivability in the conditions of unfavorable environment.

There are several reasons to structure a religious community as a system:

- role analysis. Identification in the system of primary elements: roles, interactions, different types and forms of religious behavior at the institutional and orientation levels, similar to the political communities of G. Almond;

- The system as a set of social groups and institutions, with elementary units: individuals, groups, organizations, governmental and non-governmental, pressure groups, political parties and movements, etc. (D. Easton);

- Synergetic approach, processes of self-organization of religious community can also provide an interesting solution.

Most of the researchers in the field of religion are historians, but the approach is not very suitable for risk-based social and philosophical research. It should also be noted that most authors have the church as their main institution of religious system. Templates of state and church relations are superimposed on the most complex processes with the actors of religious life, both not state and not church. Perhaps the most adequate approach would be a synergetic one. In addition, a parallel from the anthropology of Orthodox Christianity is interesting - the doctrine of synergy being developed in the philosophical horizon by S.S. Khoruzhey's laboratory. [40]

The social resonance of risk management strategies based on deep attention and even knowledge of intra- and inter-confessional processes is increasing. The most striking example is the situation at the Balakovo nuclear power plant, where an - alternative "trade union" was created by the non-traditional organization Salvation, -

---

[40] See for example: synergia-isa. ru. Accessing a resource: 30.09.10; horujy. chat. ru. Address to the resource: 30.09.10.

demanding a fair redistribution of super incomes[41]. The situation was extremely risky: the "rattling mixture" of the NPP, the New Religious Movement, alternative leadership, super incomes, and real trade union activities (conflicting in essence). As a result, the organization received a conflict, the religious leader was injured and the prosecutor's office had to intervene.

The company is approaching a new stage of modernization with the load of - potential problems[42]. It seemed that the technocratic approach would change not only the material conditions of human life, but also the structure of social relations. But social relations turned out to be not just inert, perhaps it is wrong. Many parties, primarily religious behavior of the "rebellious masses", found themselves outside the categories of rationalism. And religious communities today may not be described in vectors of reasoning, with complete rationality of actions of individual representatives of the community.

According to W. Beck: "The effect of structural changes in the forces of social agents is greater freedom from structure. And for modernization to be successful, these agents need to release themselves and actively participate in the modernization process"[43]. The result of modernization is growing individualization[44]. Religious community "saves" in the conditions of modernization from individualization, so its importance will only grow. Despite all predictions, the demand will grow, and thus, the supply will also grow. Already in quantitative terms, this supply has grown to scientific problems: from the "supermarket of religions" of the McDonaldized society to pseudo-religious terrorism. With the growth of individualization, social "atomization", the individualization of decision-making by social agents increases. Consequently, the responsibility for the decisions taken grows. This, apparently, leads to "radicalization".

The logic of religion today is inferior to the logic of religion production. The task of believers of Buddhism, for example, is not to become real Buddhists, but to become Buddhists, as the head of the Saratov community of Karma-kagyu school

---

[41] See for example: wwwcirota. www. cirota. Refer to a resource: 30.09.10; news.invictory.org. Appeal to the resource: 30.09.10.
[42] See: Grishaev, V.V. Risk and Society. - M., 2002.
[43] Beck, U. Risk Society. On the way to another art nouveau. - M., - 2000. - C. 2.
[44] See: Grishaev, V.V. Risk and Society. - M., 2002.

explains[45]. This example is very revealing. In practice we have "production" and reproduction not even of religion, but of religious behavior.

Thus, atomization undermines the foundations of socialization - basic *trust* (compared. *trust, faith derived from* "-var-" (Indo-Europe.) - to bind, connect), which is poorly described as "emotionally. Super-social motivation becomes relevant. The history of religion fully confirms the existence of this correlation between the social structure and types of religious experience[46]. According to E. Fromm: "Previously, Christianity was the religion of the poor and oppressed; the history of religious sects struggling against authoritarian political pressure shows this principle again and again in action[47]. One can disagree with the author about sects - but the correlation is underlined correctly.

Ernst Trölch and Max Weber define "church", "sect" and "cult" as the basic types of religious communities for social sciences. They were good Protestants, and Trelch is also considered a Lutheran theologian. This naturally affected the historical typology of religious communities in sociology. The fact is that the "cult" and "sect" in Lutheran theology are risky and the terms have pronounced negativity.
other estimates. Although in theology a cult is a ritual and ceremonial complex, something neutral. In 19th century Protestant German theology, the cult was identified - with Judaism, which dominated the cult. Christianity was presented as an anti-cult revolution, while the cult was a "dead religion", a formal rite[48] of worship. Trelch later criticized the American model of interaction with religious communities: Puritan and Baptist sects are individualistic, reactionary and unscientific.

According to Weber, the church is a universal organization with open membership, it can include all those who live in a certain place (the principle of canonical territory) - Orthodoxy, Catholicism, early Protestant organizations: Lutherans, Congregationalists and Presbyterians. The communities that preach -

---

[45] An open lecture by M. Glukhov. Saratov, 2010.
[46] See: Fromm, E. Psychoanalysis and Religion // Twilight of the Gods. - M., 1989.
[47] See: Ibid.
[48] See: Falikov, B.Z. Methods of studying new religious movements // Problems of teaching and the current state of religious studies in Russia. - M., 2000.

conversion are sects, even if they are Anglican, Presbyterian, and Lutheran groups, especially Baptists, Pentecostals, and especially Charisma. Conversion as exceptional creates social tension, and a source of risk. In this sense, the situation in America is - interesting - most congregations have no canonical territory and do not insist on exceptional treatment.

Richard Nibur proposed a neutral term - "denomination". Most religious organizations in the United States call themselves so. But American sociologists R. Stark and W. Bainbridge tried to rehabilitate the terms "cult" and "sect": church is a traditional conventional (ordinary) religious organization; sect is a deviant (deviant) religious organization, but with traditional beliefs and practices; finally, cult is a deviant religious organization with new beliefs and practices. At the same time, they suggested taking into account the historical factor: that today "deviation" may become "tradition" tomorrow[49]. This statement can be argued, because to become a tradition it is not enough to be "old" - there are "sects" - long-livers and cults that will never, by definition, become a tradition: "A cult can be called a weakly connected social movement that maintains unity through common submission to a charismatic leader. It contains a transcendent ideology (often but not always religious in nature) and requires a high level of devotion to culture from its members in words and deeds[50]. Most researchers dealing with new religiosity prefer to avoid old terms, preferring the acronym "NSD", the concept of "alternative religions", etc. These names are unassessed and give the phenomenon under study a presumption of innocence, which does not exclude the possibility of subsequent evaluation.

So, it is necessary to note change of structure of subjects of relations, addition of more transnational actors. A significant part of what experts are thinking about today and what the public is talking about is *risk profiling*. "Risk profiles should be reviewed and updated all the time"[51]. The most important risk profile is the religious community-, the analysis of the distribution of risk in a given environment in the current state of

---

[49] See: Ibid.

[50] Misunderstanding Cults: Searching for Objectivity in a Controversial Field, edited by Benjamin Zablocki and Thomas Robbins. - University of Toronto Press Inc, 2001. - P. 124.

[51] Giddens, E. Fate, Risk and Safety. - C. 10.

affairs and knowledge.

2.2. Religious socialization in a risk society

"Risk Society is a company producing technological and social risks. Production of risks occurs in all spheres of society's activity - economic, political, social"[52] . The sphere of religion is still a considerable gap in risk science.

The knowledge about risks in the form of metaphors and symbols contained in the words "rock", "fate", "fatal inevitability" clarify the reference points, toposes for riscology both in the study of traditionalism and in the study of alternative socialization options, which, unfortunately, are presented as a "supermarket of religions". But even to the definition of the very concept of "risk" researchers, such as W. Beck, approach with caution and do not give a final definition. One should also be more careful when defining the religious community of a risk society.

The degree of risk depends on experts and expertise[53]; this is more true for religious socialization than for other areas of public life. Experts monopolize the right to determine risk (volume, probability). In practice, the monopoly of religious expertise belongs not to professional religious scholars, but to experts, most often in the sphere of national relations.

Knowledge in religious consciousness gains new social and political meaning. The rapid "expertise" of knowledge about religion (about the risks of religious - behavior, about religious communities in a risk society) seems to mean the politicization of religion, which we have seen over the past two decades. As W. Beck suggests, in a risk society the scientific monopoly on rationality is breaking down.

The claim of theological experts to scientific rationality is indicative. This may be a weakness in adapting to the risks of religious traditionalism in general, especially Islam, which does not share theology and scientific rationality. Perhaps, there is simply no defense mechanism. Islam is often unprotected against unscrupulous examination. However, it remains an "unknown religion"; perhaps, we do not take into account many adaptive mechanisms of the Muslim Ummah. In any case, there are no absolute -

---

[52] See: Grishaev. Editorial note, op. cit. - C. 20.
[53] Bec. Op. cit. - C. 23.

authorities in the field of expert knowledge about risky processes and situations[54].

The production of risk seems to be the downside to weakening traditional religious mechanisms of "socializing danger". "Risk can be defined as systematic interaction of society with threats and dangers induced and produced by the - modernization process itself. Risks, in contrast to the dangers of past epochs, are the result of the threatening power of modernization and the feelings of uncertainty and fear it generates[55].

So, for the social dimension, the category (here it is rather a category) of "religion" measures not the truth of behavior (motivation), but the super-rationality of behavior and motivation of actors. Thus, the sphere of pseudoregionalism, quasi-religionism, and magic can be easily attributed to this category. For social philosophy, both meanings remain relevant to the analysis of risk society, especially as they relate to the production, distribution and consumption of risk. It should also be noted that the "mass" of risk is growing; consumption does not absorb risk, but accumulates it[56]. It is necessary to assess *the* results of risk production and its *latent side effects*. This is another area of searching for features of religious behavior in a risk society. "Unknown and unintended consequences become the dominant force in history and society"[57].

2.3. Risk environment for religious communities

The risk environment for the religious community seems to be the main factor of socialization. This is especially true for an outburst of fundamentalism. E. Giddens introduces the thesis: *risk creates its own environment*. Can religious communities of risk society be considered such environments, yet Giddens talks about masses? Even traditional religious communities, being stratified, seem to be hampered by the phenomenon of "mass" social religiosity. The statement "We are Russians, so we are Orthodox" is not only a problem of ethno-religious consciousness on the level of civilization slogans, but also a phenomenon of "social" religiosity.

---

[54] See: Grishaev. Editorial note, op. cit. - C. 35.
[55] Yanitsky, O.N. Ecological Movement in Russia. Critical Analysis. - Moscow: Institute of Sociology RAS, 1996. - C. 21.
[56] See: Yanitsky, O.N. Decree, op. cit.
[57] Bec. Op. cit. - C. 22.

Each of the religious communities in a risk society seems to be a specific set of minimized dangers. Interestingly, religious behavior assumes that there is no difference between subjective/objective experience of safety in a risk society, since "believer" means a coincidence of subjective and social, "my"/social. In this sense, religious community is much more convenient to study religious behavior, but this convenience easily translates into the danger of manipulation - both by "technologists" of cults and scientists.

The risk profile of modernity should include changing the profile of religious communities:

1. The risk comes from a *socialized environment*: for example, there is an invasion of human knowledge into the world of natural patterns, including the active invasion of techniques in the nature of consciousness - this is, as we know, the space of religion.

2. Development of an *institutionally recognized risk environment*, for example: anti-terrorism networks and anti-extremist programs. Risk is the basis for building these systems, rather than being random.

3. *Recognition of the existence of risk*: lack of knowledge about risk cannot be converted into "certainty" by religious or magical knowledge.

4. The *knowledge about the risk is widely distributed*: many of the dangers are known to various audiences. The preacher's task is not so much to actualize the risk and danger (the word of repentance) as to comfort.

5. *Recognition of limited expert knowledge*: no expert system can fully predict possible consequences.

Occasionally, we find the assessment of religious behavior not quite adequate among the ricologists. "In traditional cultures, riscogenic activities are more often carried out under the patronage of religion or magic. In this case the risk takes the form of uncertainty or divine predetermination of activity, and thus the risk is not recognized[58]. Magical and religious behavior of social actors does not seem to differ. The risk in conditions of predestination is not eliminated, because even in conditions of

---

[58] See: Grishaev. Editorial note, op. cit.

predestination, for example, in the notions of Islam, the responsibility of a person is not removed. In addition, religious systems, in contrast to magic systems, are a preaching of responsibility and a discourse of personal guilt.

In general, according to N. Luman, the risk puts into question the rational nature of human activity. Alternatives are being updated: the teachings of super-rational and subrational human activity, as a rule, are studied by religious studies.

It is not possible to fully measure the risk. But then what is the point in risk theories, whose concepts are related to quantitative calculation? Maybe it's just a matter of setting (as in some theories of morality) some ideal that allows you to see your own and someone else's inconsistency with the requirements of rationality[59]. The level of acceptable risk is different for those who make political decisions and those who are affected by those decisions[60]. This is all the more so in cases of religious community that do not fit, first of all, into rational structures. Secondly, religious communities in the context of globalization are an actor in international politics. After the infamous lecture at the University of Regensburg Benedict XIV, threats and words of condemnation came from all over the world: Somali Sheikh Abubakar Hassan Malin, Iraqi Sunni organization "Council of Mujahideen Shura", etc.[61] The spiritual leader of Iran, Ayatollah Ali Khamenei, accused Pope Benedict XVI of participating in the anti-Islamic crusade, the Prime Minister of the Palestinian Authority, Ismail Haniyeh also denounced the statements of a pontiff, as well as the official representative of the Pakistani Foreign Ministry, Tasnim Aslam. It was after these events that a grenade was thrown at the Orthodox Church's youth center in Gaza City, and the Anglican and Orthodox churches in the West Bank city of Nablus were attacked. The fact that Orthodox and Anglicans suffered for a lecture by the head of the Catholics (this is actually a quote from a medieval text) is also a good example.

H. Lumann proposes to implement an approach consisting in comprehending the risk phenomenon only in accordance with the meaning of communications -

---

[59] See: Luman, N. Concept of Risk // THESIS. Risk. Uncertainty. Accidence. - 1994. - № 5. - C. 135-160.
[60] See: Grishaev. Editorial note, op. cit.
[61] Maximov, Y. Why did the Pope remember the Orthodox Emperor? // http://jesuschrist.ru. Appeal to the resource: 30.09.10.

including, of course, messages about individual decisions taken[62]. Perhaps, this is the most adequate way to formalize the risk of interaction between religious communities in a rationalistic tradition. Lumann was critical of simple risk assessment: "Calculation of risk is clearly the opposite, secular situation: a program to minimize repentance[63]. Two questions arise at once: Is it not possible to be secular? Is it possible today that a non-secular situation is possible?

There is no risk-free behavior, *thus,* religious behavior is also not free from risk. Therefore, the level of responsibility and riskiness is important. Psychologists who develop issues of risk perception are criticized for striving to fully formalize the process: definitions are built "on a naive assumption that cultural prejudices (gravitation, preference) do not relate to us in our home country, as if culture is something that begins abroad, in exotic peoples[64]. According to U. Beck, the creation of new technologies leads to the production of new technological (primarily industrial) risks. Does this mean new risks for religious behavior? Apparently, it does. An example of this is the quite technological modeling of communities, the brightest example being, perhaps, the "White Brotherhood".

Rising trends in globalization are giving rise to global risks that are universal for all societies. Interestingly, most of the new religious movements insist on universalis....m. Historical religious traditionalism also presents itself as a universal religion (compare - literal translation from Latin "Catholicos" is a "universal" church). At the same time, two types of communities - "new religious movements" (NRD) and "traditional religions" - invest in global risks clearly different meaning. Perhaps, in the case of NSD, it would be more correct to talk not about universalism, but about globalism. E. Giddens believes that the risk is the result of modernization and is activated by globalization processes - does this concern religious processes? Of course it does. The word "tradition", the concept of "religious tradition" misleads those for whom the discourse is not transparent - it is not a guarantee of safety, it is not a - reservation, and it is not a universal means of protecting against risks - it is a living

---

[62] See: Luman. Op. cit.
[63] In the same place.

[64] Douglas, M. Risk as a judicial organism // Thesis. - 1994. - № 5. - C. 250.

actualization at each specific moment of time of forms of religious behavior, both "verified" and "falsified". When we talk about religious behavior, we operate with - textbook mythologists, without reporting that everything has changed long ago - this is what we constantly make sure of when we come to a religious community.

3. Giddens also explains that any action/inactivity of an individual in modern society is risky and carries the danger of unpredictable results in the future. This means for us that religious action/influence is also risky, i.e. it is unpredictable. As for the action, extremism comes to mind. Inaction is interesting because, for example, students have to prove that the thoughts 'America is to blame', 'nobody forced them...' can be overwhelmingly unpredictable. The essence of risk minimization is subtly caught by Giddens. In his opinion, "trust" is one of the possibilities of risk minimization. As it seems, if we are not talking about religion, then at least - about religious behavior.

Analysis of religious behavior requires a distinction between the concepts of risk and danger, which would be based on the nature of the observed phenomena and depend on the position of the observer. What is risk to one is danger to the other. For example, risk (as a risk resulting from a decision) may accumulate and accumulate, but for the decision maker, the danger remains constant. If we talk about measuring (parallel) religious behavior, then danger/salvation is the beginning of religion. As soon as we talk about sociology, the doctrine of salvation - we are dealing with religion. Perhaps, there is one more danger - the danger of creating by the forces of rice-cololology one more veteriology.

J. Ritzer ("McDonalization of Society") talks about the compactization of risk. One of the unforeseen consequences of total rationalization was a reduction in the size of the risk: a nuclear charge of enormous power could fit in a suitcase. Risks are compressed in the form of technology and, most importantly, expert knowledge. To create a cult today requires a personal computer and Internet access. Through the Internet, you can get into a cult, for example, a certain Oleg Malenko[65] . The social production of risk is simplified, which has not passed by the religious dimension of social relations. It should also be remembered that religious practices have a huge

---

[65] See for example: http://www.taday.ru, http://www.cirota.ru/forum.

existential "charge". To the question of "*macdonalization*" - it did not pass by the - religious communities: "...you want like this...like a hot pie...a lecture about Buddhism...". (From a conversation with representatives of a non-Buddhist community "karma-kagyu" in Saratov).

Thus, the uncertainty of risk definition in Russian science has social consequences, including in national and confessional policy, and becomes a reason for managerial manipulations. In addition, social science cannot observe society completely "from the outside"; it operates in society and is highly dependent on the situation.

2.4. Apocalyptic expectations in a risk society

Religious fundamentalism clearly answers the yes question - what to do in an era that does not recognize the highest authorities: they can be called to life again by - appealing to centuries-old religious traditions. The more this religious order is closed in itself, the easier and faster it "solves" the problem, how to live in a world where there is a choice[66].

But today these forms of fundamentalist behavior are institutionalized at the state level - the brightest option is the apocalyptic. "When it comes to risk, it means that the rational nature of human behavior is called into question[67]. Perhaps the most vivid examples of this are apocalyptic strategies, what Justin Remes calls "apocalyptic mediation" [68]or Richard Grusin "preliminary mediation" [69]- modeling the "assistant" state of affect based on eschatological scenarios of a potential future, usually apocalyptic.

Here you can trace the antithesis: "mediator/assistant", which is clearly manifested in religious communities. Obviously, totalitarian alignment of religious behavior implies a leader-mediator; whereas in free communities, the leader is an assistant. Often Christians (especially Orthodox and Catholics) hear accusations from Muslims - reducible to the idea that "a priest is a mediator", which is fundamentally wrong for most communities. Unless, of course, we are talking about deviant groups that have become isolated but mimicry for tradition, such as the Young Men in perestroika-era Russian Orthodoxy. If the helper becomes a mediator, then perhaps we can talk about a sect, a deviant religious community. We can also note a certain pattern - a society dominated by intermediary religious communities - tends to make authoritarian choices in other areas of social life.

Unfortunately, more and more often we see the phenomenon of such "mediation" in unexpected areas. Religious motivation is used at the level of global choice. The

---

[66] See: Giddens, E. Fate, Risk and Safety // THESIS. - № 5. - 1994. - C. 24.
[67] In the same place. - C. 26.
[68] Remes, J. Apocalyptic Premediations // Journal of Religion and Popular Culture. - Vol. 22(1) - Spring 2010.
[69] Grusin, R. Premediation. Criticism 46.1 (2004): 17-39.

politician and the accompanying media worker moussing an apocalyptic theme. But the problem is that there are many different ways to do it: how we do it, as humanitarians, and how we do it, for example, as political technologists, building a strategy of - mediation: "...The logic of the Bush administration can best be understood by linking it to an apocalyptic tradition. Bush, as the 'apocalyptic', used *vague* catastrophic predictions to generate *vulnerability* and fear, thus encouraging the adoption of authoritarian rules of the game without question. 1. 1. Intermediate strategy blends well with the "anti-terrorist" alarm system, especially the vivid alarm labels. The risk atmosphere in the modern era thus becomes alarming for all without exception[70][71].

Modern social policy is a chapter in the history of religion[72]. As an example, Justin Remes' research notes the extent to which evangelical religious traditions have shaped George W. Bush's strategy, especially in his dualistic outlook, his belief in divine providence, and his resistance to science (including evolutionary theory, anthropogenic global warming, and stem cell research). Bush's beliefs and social strategy were shaped by fundamentalist religious doctrines, with insufficient attention paid to Bush's ways. He is undoubtedly an apocalyptic.

Unlike prediction, apocalyptic mediation is not about the future. It is not like a weather forecast, but rather an acceleration of future scenarios that allows the "intermediary" to produce and maintain a certain level of anxiety. In other words, such mediation is not about anticipating inevitable future events, but about creating a - constant state of affect, posing as a state of risk.

Multiplication of knowledge (including rational, scientific and expert knowledge) does not reduce, but exacerbates risk awareness - in assessing the importance of this social fact, both Lumann and Giddens are united[73]. This, by the way, is a rewording of the Old Testament phrase of Ecclesiastes: "In much wisdom there is much sorrow; and who multiplies knowledge multiplies sorrow" (Ecclesiastes 1:18).

---

[70] Remes, J. Op. cit. P.112.

[71] See: Giddens E. Decree, op. cit. - C. 13.

[72] Gray, J. Black Mass: Apocalyptic Religion and the Death of Utopia. New York: Farrar, Straus and Giroux, 2007.

[73] See foreword to article: Giddens, E. Destiny, Risk and Safety. - C. 9.

However, the continuing state of affect can serve as an "emotional prevention", reducing future shocks and risks because they have already been experienced in some form. But much more interesting is mediation as a *social control tool.* By creating an image of a future disaster that could happen at any moment, a leader can unite and be supported by a frightened and agitated population seeking protection.

To see the potential power of such a strategy, we should note the Americans' response to the attacks of September 11. Intense anxiety and uncertainty forced many Americans to believe in authoritarian structures, especially political and religious ones. Support for Bush increased sharply after the terrorist attacks, and church attendance was also at its peak. Such evidence makes it clear that political and religious hegemony is often best served by public anxiety.

The text of the Apocalypse itself, the most significant apocalyptic text, has an emotional dimension. Of course, there is a critical tradition in biblistics, which binds most of the images of the book to certain events and people of the first century AD. But the book of Revelation, like all apocalyptic literature, is complex, especially what Marina Warner calls "the irrational core of the apocalyptic story... the audience *feels what's* going on. [74]This explains why many people continue to be fascinated by its content, while signs and meanings are secondary, although the text constantly talks about power. The emotional response that generates apocalyptic literature plays a major role in the endurance and power of this tradition. Such texts were often "used in support of political and social order... to pursue certain goals, political and religious in nature". [75]They seek to change affects, perhaps by moving them into *an institutional* plan.

So, we are probably only talking about affect - the experience of the End - about the powerful affect, especially it is interesting for the analysis of *mass religious behavior.* We are not talking about traditional religious forms, although they are becoming more active, but rather about authoritarian behavior, as a kind of religious behavior.

Giddens points to the discourse of death in traditional cultures, which is

---

[74] Warner, M. Angels and Engines: The Culture of Apocalypse. Raritan 25.2 (2005): 12-41. P. 23.
[75] McGinn, B. Visions of the End: Apocalyptic Traditions in the Middle Ages. 1979. New York: Columbia University Press, 1998. P. 32.

"dedicated" to talking about risk, "the link between fate and rock is death[76]. The reverse side of the exorcism of the culture of death, including burials outside the inhabited space, is again the pressure of the apocalyptic mood of the End.

Typical images of anxiety include images of all kinds of drugs that are linked to the idea of the victim - for example, in Greek. Images of wild beasts - in the American strategy, directly images of wolves were used, but it is possible to act indirectly through media images of those associated with wolves. The brightness of the law enforcers' markings would be a good option, as the military should be required to take off their uniforms and wear a ceremonial one. The easiest way to do that would be to wear a bright uniform of the DPS inspectors, as well as to prohibit hiding and oblige them to display cars with alarm markings. Unlike the military, they are the closest thing to the people. Demonstration of a nuclear explosion against this background would be a gross mistake of a manipulator. The image of a representative of state power at church service or a mosque for the scale of a single republic requires a separate interpretation. An announcement, in the end, is less interesting by conveying a message than by changing the state of the spectator's affect.

However, the mobilization of the affective component creates a certain risk. What for the average person can only cause a slight irritation, for the believer can become a warning sign and cause anxiety. As in apocalyptic literature, details remain unclear and open. As long as there is a change in affect, the facts are insignificant. Thus, it seems that many risks of religious behavior are reduced to a risk of affective behavior. Spatial-temporal compaction has "reduced" not only physical but also social distances[77]. In a religious community without social distances, the degree of interdependence increases dramatically. This is a large-scale, interdependent behavior.

Apocalyptic images simply experience and perpetuate themselves more effectively than their competitors through their own emotional power. Interestingly, unpleasant affects remain for good evolutionary reasons, emotions - such as anxiety -

---

[76] See: Giddens E. Decree, op. cit.
[77] Levashov, V.K. Globalization and social security (in Russian) // Sociis. - 2002. - № 3. - C. 19-28.

are not necessarily opposed to rational decision making, but often serve to mobilize it[78]. Since we will never be able to avoid apocalyptic moods, we can analyze them by reviewing the declared risks without giving "latency" to turn them into weapons. There is reason to believe that the forms and boundaries of "latent" weapons are far from exhausted, but we are already seeing a tendency to use religious behavior.

Eschatological representations are typical for the Middle Ages, as well as for any culture that represents a world full of dangers. Still, both experience and nature of these notions emphasizing dangers are in some respects quite different from the modern awareness of the risk of events with significant consequences. Such risk is a result of the growing process of globalization, half a century ago mankind did not experience such a threat[79].

The concept of risk becomes central in a society that says goodbye to its - traditional past. This statement applies equally to risk in an institutionalized environment as well as in other areas; the "openness" of not yet happened events reflects the resilience of the social world...[80] Practically everyone is exposed to the impact of institutionalized risk systems, regardless of whether he or she is a "person of that system". Apparently, the apocalyptic is also an important variant of risk institutionalization in modern conditions.

The difference between such institutionalized systems and other forms of risk is that in the first case, risk is rather the basis for the construction of these systems, random for them. The institutionalized risk environment connects individual and collective risk in a variety of ways. For us here, this environment is important because it can reveal how to colonize the future[81].

Interestingly, traditional institutionalized forms of religious behavior fundamentally distance themselves from the cultivation of apocalyptic moods. "Respecting the apocalyptic mystery and not deviating from its teaching, the Church

---

[78] Remes, J. Op. cit. P. 118.
[79] See: Giddens E. Decree, op. cit. 10.
[80] See: Ibid.
[81] See: Ibid.

should restrain both eschatological and maximalist sentiments of believers[82], which lead to negligence of social and civic responsibilities, and all their hoarding from "impure" (heretics) members of society. It is necessary to combine the eschatological - dimension of the church mission with an awareness of the world "here and now" as a Christian value[83].

At the same time, Christian social thought in Russia has a very modest history, in contrast to the same Catholicism. The philosophy of neotomism, as the official doctrine of the Catholic Church pours out in the Pastoral Constitution "Joy and Hope" about the Church in the modern world, adopted at the Second Vatican Council, in such a definition of "common good": "The common good includes the totality of those conditions of social life in which people, families and associations of people can more fully and quickly improve" (§ 74). While the non-philosophical doctrine of the Orthodox Church did not imply social and philosophical positions. Russian Christian philosophy remains marginal, despite colossal grants and support in this area. The main indicator - the church shop - is a place to meet with the reader, you will not find here. Pavel Florensky, neither. Sergey Bulgakov, let alone Semyon Frank - no "social" author.

The key concept here may be the solidarity of all legal strata and groups of society, including religious ones, for which we should evaluate social compromise not as a spiritual surrender and change of purity of Orthodoxy, but as a value (peacemaking) from the Christian point of view[84]. Any other position can lead to conflict and apocalyptic moods in society.

Figuratively speaking, solidarity is a projection of love into the public sphere. The development of solidarity may have a gradual character. It is important to understand that this does not threaten any "dissolution" of the Church in society, but, on the contrary, will contribute to its true mission in society. The apophatic deterrent

---

[82] For example, see: Russia before the Second Coming. Materials to the essay of Russian eschatology / Composition. C. Fomin. - Edition of the Holy Trinity Sergius Lavra, 1993.

[83] Veniamin (Novik), hegumen of Orthodoxy. Christianity. Democracy. - Aleteya, St. Petersburg, 1999. - C. 250.

[84] In the same place. - C. 251.

should prevent a cataphatic approach to reality from being reborn into a totalitarian worldview. Christian apophatism allows us to distinguish between worldview integrity and totalitarianism[85]. But for Russia, the lack of traditions of popular social philosophy is a serious problem, especially for the patriotically minded Orthodox majority.

So, "risk is a measure of danger. It combines the probability of an adverse event in the volume of that event[86][87]. In the case of an apocalyptic intermediary, the volume seems to have been exceeded, which may indicate a pseudo risk. But a pseudo risk does not explain the entire volume, otherwise waiting would not be so attractive. Unlike health hazards, the risk of being with significant consequences (high-consequence risk) by definition is not directly related to the individual...3 It is a kind of *alienated* risk. Apocalyptic mediation tells the risk with maximum consequences, thus creating an absolute alienation.

The attitude towards events with significant consequences seems to always retain a deep imprint of providentialism: "Let us live in an apocalyptic world, in the face of global dangers, but still the individual believes that governments, scientists or technicians will take the necessary measures to confront these dangers. Or he hopes that "everything will eventually work out[88].

2.5. Globalization of religious behavior risks

Risk societies are not class societies, concludes W. Beck. Religious groups have become and remain class societies to a large extent, despite all precepts and regulations. Religious groups have yet to reflect on this transition. The Russian church and the Ummah in Russia found themselves in a unique position - an extra-class of post-Soviet social perceptions. Perhaps it is their relations in Russia that will give birth to something new, necessary for a risk society.

3. Giddens and U. Bek note an increase in the number of unintended *consequences (unintended) of* social actions. Risks are getting out of control not only of individuals, but also of huge organizations, including the state, the church and the

---

[85] Veniamin (Novik). Op. cit. - C. 251.
[86] Risk management: Risk. Sustainable development. Synergetics. - M., 2000. - C. 40.
[87] See: Giddens E. Decree, op. cit. - C. 11.
[88] In the same place. - C. 18.

organizational structures of the Muslim Ummah.

The inevitability of such a situation calls into question the ontological security of a person, besides, any social action is risky[89]. Giddens believes that trust must be understood in conjunction with risk, and risk is the result of an individual's decisions. Interestingly, the only option for social practices that explicitly referred to the connection between faith (weak or strong) and risk as cause and effect are religious practices, and they have not yet been sufficiently explored by social philosophy. Whereas any social action is based on *trust in the* social system (E. Giddens). The lack of predictability of action and the lack of trust destroy the basis for social interaction[90] (E. Giddens). It is believed that the lack of predictability, but if there is trust, sociality is still preserved. Lack of faith, however, at least in the form of trust destroys all sociality.

Confidence, for example, in E. Giddens is a condition of risk reduction. If there is *trust*, there are potentially alternatives to the action. Faith is a proposal for an alternative to the present. Interestingly, in a situation of *trust, there is the* acceptance of part of the guilt.

Of course, most of the accidents, according to E. Giddens, were created by people themselves, than simply "given by God or nature. But it should be borne in mind that the risks of religious communities may be "produced" by people and recognized as such in the world of religion. But this will not stop them from being a problem of religious behavior - a question posed to science, not to law enforcement, as can be seen in the case of, for example, "recruitment" into totalitarian groups.

If people do not recognize the dangers, they are exposed to them *(run)[91]*. Another problem is whether individuals take responsibility for the risk of their actions or shift it to others. In the case of a religious community, this is a clear indicator to demarcate religiosity/pseudo-religiousity, which is increasingly referred to as mere sectarianism. It seems that the concept of 'sect', 'totalitarian sect', 'cult', etc. should be seriously revised. - Sectarianism is no longer a defining feature of pseudo-religiousity in the social dimension. Bishop of Saratov and Volsky Longin (Korchagin) well explained

---

[89] See: Grishaev. Editorial note, op. cit.
[90] See: Ibid.
[91] Giddens, E. Modernity Consequences // New post-industrial wave in the West. - M., 1999. - C. 35.

this point by the example of his confessor: "There is a very good criterion by which you can distinguish a person truly spiritual from the one who plays this spirituality willingly or unwillingly. Father Kirill is strict to himself and is unusually patient and affectionate to all others. The one who plays, on the contrary, is condescending to himself and very strict to people [92] with pseudo-religiousity there is a chance to encounter almost everywhere, even where there is no one else.

However, there is another variant of creating a "sectarian" as a social actor - hyperresponsibility, total guilt or better, all this in combination with the shifting complements the picture of pseudo-religiousity. In other words, you can shift not only on "strangers" but also on "their own".

Thus, the globalization of religious behavior risks seems to be primarily an increase in *intensity*:

    - For example, the intensification of negative processes among religious communities as collective subjects of religious behavior;

    - increase in events with significant consequences, such as the terrorist threat.

Globalization of risk can also be understood in the sense of a *proliferation of random events* that affect everyone or at least a large *number of* people: for example, changes in the global division of religious affiliation. The local control mechanism may be disrupted by absorbing the decay products of all those who used these resources.

---

[92] Longin (Korchagin), ep. Man can not live without God: articles, talks, answers to questions. - Saratov: Publishing House of the Saratov Diocese, 2010. - C. 159.

CONCLUSION

Religious community in "statics" is the area of coincident algorithms of - behavior in overcoming neurotic states, coincident points of reference in the basic cognitive activity - the realization of the ability of the imagination, the community of positive exit and ultimate benefits. Interestingly, the religious community - a phenomenon "metaphysical" in the literal sense - indicates a social action "in eternity," in other words, the reference points are outside the usual perception of space and time. The reference points make it a recovering community - the return particle "re-" indicates a returnable social action. But in its dynamics, religious commonality is a fundamental risk-society based on the unity of ideas about sin as a universal dimension, and it defines the dimension of commonality. The category of sin has "catalogued" not only the intuitive and socially acquired propensities of the individual to risk, but even ontological situations.

So, risk is a category that is quite applicable and even necessary in studying the *dynamics of* religion in the modern world. Risk is a "measure of all things" of the XXI century, including religious communities. An interesting research perspective is indicated by u. Beck: "There is a general nature of political odds and contradictions inherent in a global society of risk: in an era when faith in God, classes, nation or government disappears, the recognized and recognized global nature of threats becomes a source of connections in the face of which the seemingly indestructible constants of the political world suddenly soften and are made malleable for reincarnation[93]. It seems that if faith in God disappears first, according to Beck, then it is also to be recreated, at least as the reconstruction of a categorical unity of measurement of religious communities in a risk society.

As a perspective of the research we will designate a number of topics:

1. Concepts of religious behavior risks.

2. Everyday occurrence of ontological risk in the system of religious behavior.

---

[93] Beck, U. Address in the State Duma of the Russian Federation. 28 November 2001 // www.academy-go.ru. Address to the resource: 30.09.10.

3. Philosophical model of risk society and the social concept of the Russian Orthodox Church.
4. Islamization in social-philosophical discourse of a risk society.
5. Network risks of religious behavior.
6. Sacrifice as *religious* behavior.
7. The threat of terror in the philosophical discourse of a risk society.

Basic terms:

Risk *is a* behavioral reaction (making a decision in a situation of choice) provided that an adverse event is likely to occur.

Ontological risk is an absolute value of negative consequences for the subject of choice.

Altruistic behavior - a situational resolution of the risk situation in favor of social behavior (comparison with "organic solidarity")[94].

Sin - deviant behavior in religious systems. In Christian consciousness, "sin" is never limited to stating the negative consequences of any disgraceful (ethically or socially) act, but prolongs these consequences in an arithmetical progression for the future (compare M. Douglas's position)[95].

Symbolic exchange is a functional distortion of the victim's idea in modern social anthropology.

Sacrifice - "symbolic healing" (compare Greek "facmakos" - cure); filling the integrity through the "cure" (the link between man and the world). The cure - "substance", which contributes to the normalization of the system of exchange with the world. Already the ancient world has distorted the idea of the victim as a cure that normalizes exchange, replacing it with a simple exchange. Christian concepts of the Eucharistic sacrifice seem to be an attempt to restore the idea of the sacrifice as a cure.

Interiorization - the doctrine is known to believers and perceived as a system of their own "inner" values, is the foundation of their "inner" religiosity. The system of religious socialization leads to the development of patterns of "internal" religiosity.

Love is a belief that is accompanied by enthusiasm (experiencing an intense reaction caused by the action of secretion glands, nerves, muscles and a simultaneous weakening of the dominant stimulus) (D. Trout). [96]

According to D. Trout, ***religious behavior*** is a means of reproducing reactions that guarantee the achievement of the goal; it can be found almost everywhere, in all

---

[94] Durkheim, E. The Elementary Forms of the Religious Life. - London, - 1976. - P. 11.
[95] Douglas, M. Risk Acceptability According to the Social Sciences. N.Y., - 1985. - P. 15-17.
[96] Цит. по: Wulff, D.M. Psyhology of Religion: Classic and Contemporary Views. - N. Y., - 1997. - P. 112. - P. 114-115.

living organisms. They can react differently to objects of ants and chimpanzees, erudite and savage, woman and man, child and parent. But their reaction will be religious if it is *aimed at some positive goals*, and also has the necessary degree of intensity. If an individual acts *automatically,* without enthusiasm, his behavior is non-religious. This is not an integrated movement in the future, it does not include hope and expectations[97].

A *religious act* is any action that is perceived as complementary to the *ways to achieve a goal that* seems most valuable to the individual. The most religious can be considered reactions that develop the highest intensity of reproduction, and subjectively experience as faith, hope, love[98].

Religious norms and images - are the guarantors of achieving a goal that is otherwise unattainable - understanding, shelter, peace, sex or food. Thus, mistakenly characterize religious notions as illusion, autistic or pathological views. If the development of science and technology will destroy this *essential technique of adaptation*, they will also create a new "faith of scientists". Scientific behavior can be considered no less religious because it implies achieving positive goals.

Faith:

1) a circumstance that explains the probability of any behavior to be expected;
2) a by-product of behavior regarding past events;
3) the usual way of explaining sustainable behavior when ignoring the surrounding events that supported it[99].

The list of literature:

1. Douglas, M. Risk Acceptability According to the Social Sciences. - N.Y., - 1985.
2. Durkheim, E. The Elementary Forms of the Religious Life. - London, - 1976.
3. Huntington, S., The Clash of Civilization. - N.Y., - 1996.
4. Skinner, B.F. Beyond Freedo and Dignity. - N.Y., - 1971.
5. Wells, W.R. The Biological Foundation of Beliefs. - S.L. - 1921.
6. Wulff, D.M. Psyhology of Religion: Classic and Contemporary Views. - N.Y., - 1997.

---

[97] See: Ibid.
[98] See: Ibid.
[99] Skinner, B.F. Beyond Freedo and Dignity. - N. Y., - 1971. - P. 99, 368.

7. Altermatt, U. Ethno-nationalism in Europe. - M., - 2000.

8. Bakhach, O. Social Justice in Islam // www.islam.ru/lib. Address to the resource: 09.02.10.

9. Beck, U. Address in the State Duma of the Russian Federation. 28 November 2001 // www.academy-go.ru. Address to the resource: 30.09.10.

10. Beck, U. Cosmopolitan Society and its Enemies // Journal of Sociology and Social Anthropology, - 2003. - vol. VI. - № 1 (21);

11. Beck, U. Risk Society. On the way to another art nouveau. - M., - 2000.

12. Weber, M. Protestant Sects and the Spirit of Capitalism. - M., - 1990.

13. Veniamin (Novik), hegumen of Orthodoxy. Christianity. Democracy. - Aleteya, St. Petersburg, - 1999.

14. Giddens, E. Modernity Consequences // New post-industrial wave in the West. - M., 1999. - C. 35.

15. Giddens E. Fate, Risk and Safety // THESIS No. 5. 1994.

16. Grishaev, V.V. Risk and Society. - M., 2002.

17. Other publications on religious risks.

18. Douglas, M. Risk as a judicial organism // Thesis. - 1994. - № 5. - C. 250.

19. Duplinskaya, Yu.M. Ontological basis of differences between theology and philosophy // Pimenov Readings. - Saratov, - 2007.

20. Karpov, A.V. Psychology of group decisions. - M., - 2000.

21.Longin (Korchagin), ep. Man can not live without God: articles, talks, answers to questions. - Saratov: Publishing House of the Saratov Diocese, 2010. - C. 159.

22.Lossky, V.N. Essay of Mystical Theology of the Eastern Church. M., 1991.

23. Luman, N. The Concept of Risk // THESIS, - 1994, - vol. 5. - P. 5. 157.

24.Luman, N. Power / Per. with him. A. Y. Antonovsky. - Moscow: Praxis, 2001. - — 256 c.

25.Maximov, Y. Why did the Pope remember the Orthodox Emperor? // http://jesuschrist.ru. Appeal to the resource: 30.09.10.

26.Malashenko, A.V. Vremya South: Russia in Chechnya, Chechnya in Russia (together with Dmitry Trenin), - M., - 2002.

27. Malashenko, A.V. Islam for Russia. - M., - 2007.

28.Malashenko, A.V. Islamic Alternative and Islamist Project. - M., - 2006.

29. Malashenko, A.V. Islamic landmarks of the North Caucasus. - M., - 2001.

30. Malashenko, A.V. How they were chosen in Chechnya. - M., - 2006.

31.Maslow, A. New frontiers in human development // Chrestomatics on humanistic psychotherapy. - M., - 1995.

32.Maslow, A. Self-actualization // Psychology of personality (Texts). - M., - 1982.

33. Mikhailov, A.V. Heidegger. A man in the world. - M., - 1990.

34. Nemesiye Emessky. About human nature. - M., 1996.

35.Risk society and man in the XXI century: alternatives and development scenarios. Saratov, 2006. (Section 6: People and Religions in a Risk Society).

36.Odessa, M., Feldman D. Terror as an ideologeme (to the history of development) // social sciences and modernity. - 1994. - № 6.

37.Orlov, M. Religion in Risk Society // Risk Society: management strategies and alternative ways of thinking. Saratov, 2009.

38.Risk society: management strategies and alternative thinking styles (in Russian) / Ed. by Ustiantseva V.B., Orlov M.O., Pod. Saratov, 2009.

39.Orlov, M.O. Risks of global dynamics: religion and terrorism // www.ru. Address to the resource: 04.02.10.

40.Basics of the social concept of the Russian Orthodox Church // http://www.ru. Address to the resource: 09.02.10.

41.Pashkevich, I.L. Virtual dimension of terrorism // Virtual space of culture. Saratov, 2008.

42.Thoreau, L. The Future of Capitalism. How today's economic forces are shaping tomorrow's world. - Novosibirsk, 1999.

43.Ustiantsev, V.B. Civilization concepts of risk society (in Russian) // Theses of reports and speeches of the IV Russian Philosophical Congress. - T. 3. M, 2005. - C. 632.

44.Ustiantsev, V.B. Systemic risks in formation of the global world // Philosophy, man, civilization: new horizons of the XXI century. Ч. 1. - Saratov, 2004. - C.

97-102.

45. Ustiantsev, V.B. Concepts of risk society // Philosophy, man, civilization: new horizons of XXI century. Ч. 2. - Saratov, 2004. - С. 181-186.

46. Ustiantsev, V.B. Imperative of social justice // Law, man, justice: philosophical and legal problems. - Saratov: GOU VPO SSAP Publishing House // Law, man, justice: philosophical and legal problems. - 2004. - С. 121-124.

47. Ustiantsev, V.B. Person, life space, risks: value and institutional aspects. - Saratov, 2006. - 184 с.

48. Ustiantsev, V.B. Risk anthropology: conceptual bases // Risk society and man: ontological and value aspects. - Saratov: Science, 2006. - С. 224-241.

49. Ustiantsev, V.B. Space of civilizations in the context of change of rationality types // Philosophy and society. - 2007. - № 3. - С. 81-98.

50. Ustiantsev, V.B. Horizons of human ambivalence in the risk society (in Russian) // Science. Philosophy. Society. Materials of the V Russian Philosophy Congress. - T. 3. Novosibirsk, - 2009. - С. 283.

51. Ustiantsev, V.B. Institutional man and order in discourses of types of rationality // Human world: normative dimension. - Saratov, 2009. - С. 35-39.

52. Risk management: Risk. Sustainable development. Synergetics. - M., - 2000.

53. Falikov, B.Z. Methods of studying new religious movements // Problems of - teaching and the current state of religious studies in Russia. - M., 2000.

54. Fedotova, V.G. Terrorism: from old to new // Philosophical sciences, - 2003. - № 2. - С. 25.

55. Frank, S.L. Reality and man. - M., - 1997.

56. Frankle, V. Man in search of meaning. - M., 1990.

57. Fromm, E. Psychoanalysis and Religion // Twilight of the Gods. - M., - 1989.

58. Fromm, E. Types of religion and religious experience // Religion and society: Sociology of religion. - M., - 1996.

59. Heidegger, M. Question about technology // Heidegger, M. Time and being. - M., - 1993.

60. Chesterton, G.K. The Eternal Man. - M., - 1991.

61. Young, K. The problem of the soul of our time. - M., - 1994.

62. Jung, K. Man and its meaning. - M., 1996.

63. Yanitsky, O.N. Ecological Movement in Russia. Critical Analysis. - Moscow: Institute of Sociology RAS, 1996. - C. 21.

More
Books!

OMNIScriptum

Printed by Books on Demand GmbH, Norderstedt / Germany